BR PASSENGER SECTORS IN COLOUR

For the Modeller and Historian

David Cable

CONTENTS

Title Page: The 'Royal Ascot' headboard is mounted on the front of No 47809 *Finsbury Park* which negotiates the junction at Wokingham with its special from Liverpool to Ascot on Ladies' Day in June 1992. Note the coaching stock and the black-backed nameplate on the locomotive which is in the second IC scheme.

Above: An unidentified Class 43 brings its HST round the bend by Brunel's pumping station at Starcross early one morning in May 1990. The sea is like a mirror. The train is the first Plymouth to Paddington of the day, and life is pleasant!

MIX
Paper from
responsible sources
FSC® C014615

First published 2012

ISBN 978 0 7110 3441 9

Published by Ian Allan Publishing
An imprint of Ian Allan Publishing Ltd, Hersham,
Surrey KT12 4RG

Visit the Ian Allan website at
www.ianallanpublishing.com

Distributed in the United States of America and
Canada by BookMasters Distribution Services.

INTRODUCTION

This book deals with passenger services from 1983 – when separate cost centres were introduced – up to 1996 and the start of the restructuring of British Rail into separate private companies and franchises. Because of the large degree of overlap in regard to motive power usage, it also includes parcels activities. It complements the publication dealing with Railfreight throughout the same period.

The book outlines the rolling stock history throughout this period, the services operated, the type of stock used on the major services, and the locomotive classes and multiple-units used per sector. The bulk of the book, however, deals with the sector colour schemes of locomotives and multiple-units, but not hauled rolling stock which is more than adequately covered in the companion volumes to this publication.

Successive governments, abetted by the dead hand of the short-sighted Treasury, had restricted investment in the railways in favour of road transport, affecting the passenger sector just as much as the freight sector. Compounded by above-inflation-level fare increases in so many cases, and the ups and downs of the economy, it was no surprise that the withdrawal of passengers from trains into their own cars became one of the factors that led to the need to examine the finances of British Rail. These had been dependent over many years on subsidies from governments that never considered the value provided by the railway as a public service – never mind the effects of pollution. Well, things never change, do they?!

The limitations of government finance restricted these sectors in providing all that their customers sought in terms of reliable, cheap transport. The long-suffering passengers, especially commuters, had to rely at the outset of this period mainly on ageing passenger stock, and it was only towards the later part of sectorisation that new stock was widely introduced in the form of Class 90 and 91 locomotives, Mark 4 passenger coaches, and several multiple-unit designs. This, together with the efforts of the various Passenger Transport Executives (PTEs), brought about a gradually improving image of the railway, as colour schemes broke away from the old, all-pervading and rather shabby BR corporate blue. Even then, much of the new equipment was below current state-of-the-art specification compared with what was being applied in Europe.

Furthermore, major improvements in track work during the period only comprised the extension of electrification from Colchester to Norwich, and the on-the-cheap ECML electrification. And the other side of the coin included simplification of track layouts, leading to resultant operating complications and increased unreliability of passenger services.

It is true that privatisation has improved matters for most passenger services, but it is also true that British Rail would have done the same, given the huge investment that has been forthcoming since 1996. I therefore express my appreciation for the efforts made by all BR staff to keep services operating as well as they did (and still do) under trying conditions and shoestring budgets.

The book illustrates the various classes of locomotives and multiple-units that have operated within each of the different sectors in their own sector colour schemes, including a few that were painted in special colours before sectorisation but performed most of their duties after the change: for example, those in Great Western green. A few pictures of locomotives from other sectors working passenger services are shown, as are locomotives and multiple-units painted in special colours where they are working regular scheduled services. Space precludes being able to show pictures of enthusiasts' special trains, whether with everyday or preserved haulage power. London Underground, Docklands Light Railway and other such systems are outside the remit of this publication.

The photographs in each section are presented in class number sequence and were (with one exception) taken by myself; apart from some of mine used by Colour-Rail, they are unpublished until now. I have tried to include pictures from as wide a variety of locations as possible, but in order to provide as much detail for modellers some views are repetitive because they are of interesting locations, or are where particular classes primarily worked. Any not in the public domain were taken with appropriate permission. I do not record specific dates or train numbers, and have no objection to pictures which are back lit.

The book deals specifically with the colour schemes during this period, and is aimed at the modeller and historian. It does not, and is not intended to, go into details of the design of rolling stock.

Finally, as ever, I would like to express my sincere appreciation for the efforts of the Ian Allan crew. Thank you everyone.

David Cable
Hartley Wintney 2011

SECTORISATION TO PRIVATISATION

Prior to 1983, British Rail had operated within an overall corporate budget supplemented by substantial subsidies from the government. But this ever-increasing supplement was challenged by the Thatcher government and the Treasury, leading to an examination into the justification for such expenditure, bearing in mind that the Restructuring of British Railways report under Dr Beeching had been intended to put the system on a better financial basis. This examination resulted in the establishment of separate cost centres which reflected the various sectors of the railway system.

Below: The APT had pioneered the Inter City scheme when it was introduced in 1981, although when introduced to the fleet it was modified in some details. No 370003 leads this Glasgow to Euston extra service past Carpenders Park in April 1985. The two power cars in the centre of the train carry the BR double arrow logo and APT respectively. Note the full set number at front spoiler level, and the inscription 'Inter City' with the BR logo and APT in black outline either side. The red and white stripes and dark grey band are carried over the roof.

Passenger, parcels and freight operations plus departmental activities were split, the passenger operations being further subdivided. But prior to this, two passenger activities had already been identified, for marketing purposes, as somewhat separate from the main basic system, namely Inter City and ScotRail. These were maintained under sectorisation together with other subdivisions, so that the structure became:

Inter City
London & South East, becoming
    Network South East
Provincial Railways, later
    Regional Railways
ScotRail
Parcels and Mail
Railfreight and Departmental (covered
    in a separate book).

Before the period under review, various government proposals had provided for the establishment of Passenger Travel Executives in major cities apart from London. These were based on the conurbations of Glasgow (Greater Glasgow/Strathclyde), Newcastle upon Tyne (Tyneside/Tyne & Wear), Leeds (West Yorkshire), Manchester (SELNEC/Greater Manchester), Liverpool (Merseyrail), Birmingham (West Midlands) and Sheffield (South

Yorkshire), although the latter, unlike the others, did not adopt specific rolling stock liveries for its operating area apart from one short-lived DMU.

In the first instance, the Gatwick Express operation was incorporated within the Inter City sector, but in 1994 was branded as a specific subdivision with its own colours. Thameslink also broke away from Network South East. The other major passenger activity introduced during the period was, of course, Eurostar, which operated quite independently from the main BR system, but has been included so as to cover all main line passenger operations in this period.

All of these sectors had their own individual colour schemes, and to those who had lived through the increasingly shabby BR corporate blue era these were like a breath of fresh air. There had been one major exception to the blue era, when in 1981, the APT was finished in the so-called Executive livery, followed by the coaching stock for the resuscitated 'Manchester Pullman'. This livery subsequently was adopted as the basis for the Inter City scheme.

Apart from the PTEs and Eurostar, all other passenger and parcels operations were taken over by the private franchises from 1996 onwards, and the lost colour schemes of these companies are illustrated in the companion book dealing with this aspect.

OUTLINE OF ROLLING STOCK HISTORY

At the introduction of sectorisation in 1983, much of the rolling stock was formed of locomotives, coaches and multiple-units which had emanated from the 1955 British Railways Modernisation Plan and the first phase of overhead electrification on the West Coast Main Line. Locomotives for passenger and parcels services comprised diesel Classes 31, 33, 37, 40, 45 and 46, several with relatively poor power-to-weight ratios, and electric Classes 81 and 85 covering the West Coast Main Line. The well-known passenger Class 52 'Westerns' and Class 55 'Deltics' had also been introduced but had been withdrawn before sectorisation.

Five other major passenger locomotive classes were subsequently introduced in addition to the initial 1955-era designs before sectorisation was announced. The diesel mixed-traffic Class 47 and the Class 50, the mixed-traffic electro-diesel Class 73 for Gatwick Express services, and two new electric classes – the 86s and 87s on the West Coast Main Line – were all seen in action. In particular, the introduction of the IC125 high-speed Class 253/4 with Class 43 locomotives on each end made a major impact on express passenger trains on certain lines.

Multiple-units after 1955 were formed of the original 101 to 128 diesel classes, Classes 302 to 315 overhead and Classes 411 to 423 third rail electric units, plus a few miscellaneous units. (Classes such as the 405 4SUBs were, of course, pre-1955 designs.) New second generation multiple-units were also starting to be introduced by the time sectorisation was promulgated – the Pacers and Class 150 DMUs, Classes 317 and 318 OHE EMUs and the Class 455 DC EMUs.

During the sectorisation period up to privatisation, many more new designs of multiple-units were commissioned, plus the Class 90 and 91 electric locomotives. The Class 90s were introduced to replace many Class 86s on the WCML, which were either transferred to East Anglia routes or re-geared for freight/intermodal services. The Class 91 was introduced when the ECML line from King's Cross, initially to Leeds and then throughout to Edinburgh, was electrified. Loco-hauled coaches and parcels stock were, in the main, introduced before sectorisation, and only the Mark 4 stock on the ECML was introduced during the period under review.

Whilst more multiple-units have been designed and put into operation since privatisation, as far as passenger locomotives are concerned only the Class 57s rebuilt from Class 47s, and the Class 67s, primarily introduced for the now lost high-speed parcels services, have been seen. Large numbers of passenger sector locomotives have been withdrawn during both the sectorisation and the privatisation period due to the need for passenger trains to combine locomotives with driving trailers at each end of the train so as to reduce the number of expensive engines with cheap trailers, as well as reducing light engine movements at termini, but in particular with the emphasis for passenger services to be comprised of multiple-units.

ROLLING STOCK AND SERVICES IN THE SECTORISATION PERIOD

At the outset of sectorisation after 1983, passenger train services were operated in the general manner described below. Electrification was already established throughout the greatest part of Southern Region (third rail). The 25kV West Coast Main Line electrification was complete, together with the associated suburban networks in Birmingham, Manchester, Liverpool and Glasgow, plus the third rail Mersey system and most North London Lines. Inner and outer suburban services from Liverpool Street and King's Cross were well established, but the extension to Norwich and the whole East Coast Main Line schemes had yet to commence, although by the introduction of privatisation these were in full operation.

All of the above lines were operated either by electric locomotive-hauled coaching stock, or by electric multiple-units (EMUs). The remainder of the BR system was worked by diesel locomotives with coaching stock, or by diesel multiple-units (DMUs).

A selection of the more important routes is given below, indicating the type of rolling stock normally working the route during sectorisation up to privatisation.

West Coast Main Line: Class 86 and Class 87 locomotives and later Class 90s with predominantly Mark 3 coaches. The introduction of Driving Trailers released many Class 86s for transfer to other lines and services.

East Coast Main Line: IC125s but superseded by Class 91 locomotives initially with Mark 3 coaching stock, later replaced with Mark 4 coaches, except for services north of Edinburgh which were worked by IC125 diesel units.

Liverpool Street to East Anglia: Initially Class 47 locomotives with Mark 2 stock. Norwich services were replaced by Class 86 locomotives cascaded from the WCML. These were replaced after privatisation by cascaded Class 90s and Mark 3 coaching stock. Cambridge/King's Lynn services were replaced by EMUs.

Midland Main Line: IC125s.

Cross Country: Class 47s with Mark 2 coaches, with Class 86s working north of Birmingham on the WCML. IC125s were used mainly on services to/from the West of England.

Below: No 47612 *Titan* had taken over from No 85006 which brought the Manchester to Brighton express down the WCML. The scene is at Mitre Bridge, Willesden, in May 1989, with the small signal arm giving the road. Standard InterCity livery with black headcode panel.

Right: A pleasant line-up on Crewe South shed in May 1993 sees No 37429 in Regional Railways colours, No 47706 in de-labelled ScotRail, No 47715 *Haymarket* in Network South East scheme 2, and an unidentified RES Class 90.

Brighton/Portsmouth to South Wales: Class 33s with Mark 1 coaching stock, but replaced by Class 155/158 DMUs.

Paddington to South Wales: IC125s.

Paddington to West of England: Class 50s (some Class 47s) with Mark 2 coaches, but gradually replaced by IC125s.

Waterloo to Exeter: Class 50s with Mark 2 coaches. On withdrawal of Class 50s, Class 47s relocated from Scotland operated the trains until replaced by Class 159 DMUs.

Waterloo to Bournemouth/Weymouth: Class 432 4 REP EMUs with Class 438 4TC trailers and Class 33s working push-pull west from Bournemouth. In conjunction with electrification to Weymouth, Class 442 EMUs worked the services throughout. When Class 432 power cars were being withdrawn to provide electric motors for Class 442s, Class 73 locomotives worked the services with either a loco replacing one power car of a Class 432 or with one or two Class 73s hauling Class 438 trailers.

Cardiff to Crewe: Class 37 locomotives with a mixture of Mark 1 and Mark 2 coaches.
Class 33s also worked these services for a while.

Manchester to North Wales: Class 37s and some Class 47s with Mark 2 coaches. WCML trains to Holyhead were worked by Class 47s from Crewe.

Hull/Cleethorpes to Manchester/ Liverpool: Mainly Class 31 locomotives with Mark 2 coaching stock, although Class 47s were fairly common.

Norwich to Birmingham: Class 31s with Mark 2 coaches.

Settle and Carlisle: Class 37s and 47s with Mark 2 coaches. These were replaced by Class 156 DMUs.

Newcastle upon Tyne to Liverpool: Class 47s with Mark 2 coaches.

Glasgow to Edinburgh/Aberdeen: Class 47/7s with Mark 2 coaches in push-pull mode.

North and West of Scotland: Class 37s with Mark 1 and Mark 2 coaches.

London to Kent Coast: Class 411/412 EMUs with Class 419 luggage vans for boat trains.

London to South Coast: Class 421/422/423 EMUs.

Gatwick Express: Class 73s with Class 489 driving luggage vans and Mark 2 coaches.

All other services were worked by appropriate locomotives, DMUs and EMUs.

PASSENGER AND PARCELS SECTORS LOCOMOTIVE CLASSES

Locomotives used by these sectors were originally classified by type relating to horsepower; the notes below categorise the various classes in a similar sequence. Each class is identified with the various sectors within which it was allocated, although there were inevitable occasions when a particular situation involved the use of a locomotive from a different sector, including freight and departmental locomotives and workings, a few of which are illustrated.

Some of the classes were towards the end of their withdrawal; they worked some of their last days for certain sectors, but were never an official part of them. They are marked with an asterisk.

It is important to note that the term 'Mainline' refers to the original description of a colour scheme similar to that of Inter City, but without the Inter City brand inscription. It does not refer to the subsequent use by the freight sector of the blue scheme called Mainline.

Class Sectors

08/09	Inter City, Network South East, Provincial/Regional, Parcels
20*	Provincial/Regional (limited)
26*	Provincial/Regional (limited)
31	Mainline, Provincial/Regional
33	Network South East (also loaned for some Provincial services)
37	Mainline, Provincial/Regional
40*	Provincial/Regional (limited)
43	Inter City
45/46*	Provincial/Regional (limited), Parcels
47	Inter City, Mainline, ScotRail, Network South East, Parcels/RES
50	Inter City, Network South East
73	Mainline, Network South East, Gatwick Express, Merseyrail
81*	Parcels, extra passenger trains
85*	Parcels, extra passenger trains
86	Inter City, Network South East, Parcels/RES
87	Inter City
89	Inter City
90	Inter City, Mainline, Parcels/RES
91	Inter City

The Merseyrail Class 73 is included for completeness of that PTE, although it is not known ever to have undertaken passenger duties.

Right: In NSE scheme 1 colours, Class 117 L428 approaches Ash with a Reading to Tonbridge stopping service in May 1987. Another of those pleasant locations now ruined by a netted-in footbridge.

PASSENGER COACHES, VANS AND MULTIPLE-UNITS

At the start of sectorisation, coaching stock was formed of either Mark 1, 2 or 3 designs. Mark 4 designs were introduced during sectorisation. Mark 1 coaches were constructed using a chassis as a base on which the body was mounted, whilst the other three classes were of monocoque construction.

Numbers of doors changed over time. Mark 1 stock had at least three hinged doors per side, and with Southern Region high-capacity units there were doors for every compartment. But with Mark 2, 3 and 4 designs the number of doors was reduced to provide extra body strength but at the cost of passengers on mainline coaches entering and leaving quickly. With the exception of the Class 442 Mark 3 design, other new multiple-units adopted sliding doors, two sets per side, which enabled better passenger movements but not retention of heat in cold weather.

All passenger coaches were mounted on 4-wheel bogies using combinations of leaf and/or coil springing, with air bag suspension being used particularly on more modern rolling stock. Mark 1 and 2 and many Mark 3 coaches were built with seats aligned with windows. However, in more recent times, Mark 3 and Mark 4 coach bodies were built/ rebuilt to one standard for cost economies, windows being set to suit the pitch of seats in First Class, leaving Standard Class sets to be misaligned with windows in many cases.

Parcels and mail rolling stock was primarily formed of Mark 1 stock, although a few Mark 2 vans were used. In certain areas, 4-wheel CCT vans were also used. Vans were of a variety of designs, some being pure parcels brake vans, with others specifically designed for handling BRUTE trolleys etc. In the 1990s, some vans were redesigned to incorporate a driving cab to enable push-pull working, particularly for trains routed in and out of the Wembley Royal Mail terminal.

All multiple-units had mandatory yellow ends. Apart from a few residual passenger and multiple-unit coaches in plain blue, the bulk of coaching stock at the start of sectorisation was in blue and grey. Over time this was repainted into the appropriate sector or PTE colours. Parcels and mail vans used a variety of colours – plain blue, blue and grey, red, red with two thin gold bands, and Inter City.

For further details, the companion books in this series, which cover this subject more fully, are recommended.

PASSENGER AND PARCELS CLASSES PER SECTOR

It should be noted that some locomotives and multiple-units retained their original blue or blue and grey schemes throughout most, if not all, of the period under review. Of particular note are the passenger Class 33s, of which only two received NSE colours, and then only at the end of sectorisation.

Classes per Sector

Inter City	08; 43; 47; 73; 86; 87; 89; 90; 91; 97; 370; 489
Mainline	31; 37; 47; 73; 90
ScotRail	47/4; 47/6; 47/7
London & South East	309; 411; 419; 421
Network South East	*Locomotives*: 08; 09; 33; 47; 50; 73; 86; 97 *DMUs*: 101; 104; 108; 115; 117; 119; 121; 122; 159; 165; 166 *DEMUs*: 205; 207

	EMUs: 302; 307; 308; 309; 310; 312; 313; 315; 317; 319; 321; 365; 411; 412; 413; 415; 416; 419; 421; 422; 423; 431; 432; 442; 455; 456; 465; 466; 482; 483; 485; 486; 487 *MISC*: 930; 931; 960
Provincial Regional	*Locomotives*: 08; 31; 37 *DMUs*: 101; 122; 142; 143; 150; 151; 153; 155; 156; 158 *EMUs*: 304; 305; 310
Parcels/RES/ Royal Mail	08; 47; 86; 90; 114; 302; 325; 419
PTEs	*Strathclyde*: 101; 107; 156; 303; 314; 318; 320 *Tyne & Wear*: 142; 143; *West Yorkshire*: 141; 144; 155; 158; 307; 308; 321 *South Yorkshire*: 108 *Greater Manchester*: 142; 150; 303; 305; 323; 504 *Merseyrail*: 73; 142; 150; 501; 507; 508 *West Midlands*: 150; 312; 323
Thameslink	319
Others	Eurostar: 373 Stansted Express: 322 Network North West: 150 Gatwick Express: 73; 489

PASSENGER NAMEPLATES AND LOGOS

Locomotive nameplates were generally of standard BR cast metal design using normal case lettering, apart from a period prior to privatisation when Class 43 power cars were fitted with stainless steel plates. The Class 50s and four Class 47s painted in GW green in commemoration of GW150 in 1985 carried typical Great Western Railway type case for both their nameplates and cast number plates. Supplementary badges and crests were carried in many cases.

Names were varied and are summarised as follows:

Class 33	Burma connections (passenger sector only)
Class 37/4	Scottish and Welsh connections
Class 43	Places; counties; organisations; persons
Class 47	Persons; places; organisations; Scottish connections; words beginning with Res (parcels sector)
Class 50	Warships
Class 73	Southern connections
Class 86	Cities; organisations; persons; LNWR connections; newspapers
Class 87	Historical persons; cities; Scottish connections
Class 90	Organisations; media connections; postal connections
Class 91	Persons; miscellaneous items
Class 442	Southern connections.

Quite apart from nameplates, Network South East branded its stock in NSE colours with logos representing the lines on which the rolling stock worked, primarily multiple-units but including a few locomotives as well.

Below: The NSE North London Lines logo was originally entitled Harlequin Line, representing Hatch End, Harlesden and Queens Park.

The lines were identified as below, each having its own design of logo to relate to some aspect of its area of operation:

Anglia Electrics	Bedford-Bletchley
Chiltern Line	Chiltern Turbo
Essex Electrics	Great Eastern
Great Northern Line	Island Line
Kent Coast	Kent Link
London, Tilbury & Southend	Marks Tey-Sudbury
Marsh Link	Northampton Line
North Downs	North London Lines
Oxted Line	Portsmouth Express
Solent & Wessex	South Hants
South London Lines	South Western Lines
South Western Turbo	Sussex Coast
Thames	Thames Link
Thames Turbo	Thames Turbo Express
Three Counties	Uckfield Line
Waterloo & City	Wessex Electrics
West Anglia	West of England
1066 Country	Ride the 1066 route

Others were devised but not used, e.g. Windsor Line.

A further logo was applied to a limited number of Class 421 EMUs, inscribed 'Capital Coast Express', which were boosted to give 100mph capability on Victoria to Brighton services.

Various miscellaneous multiple-units carried names at one time or another, some official and some as depot initiatives. A few RES (Rail Express Systems) locomotives carried a brass cut-out of a Cheshire cat, the Railfreight depot emblem for Crewe South loco shed, under the nearside driver's cab window. Many blue locomotives based in Scotland had been decorated with white Scottish terriers representing Eastfield depot, or black and yellow Highland stags for Inverness depot, and these were also applied to locomotives in ScotRail Blue and some Scottish-based Inter City locomotives. A few Thornaby locomotives carried white kingfisher shed logos.

Examples of some nameplates and NSE logos are shown in the book.

PASSENGER AND PARCELS LIVERY DETAILS

In all cases rolling stock had mandatory yellow front ends of varying sizes. Roofs were black unless stated otherwise. Standard yellow cantrail bands identified First Class accommodation, with a red cantrail band for restaurant facilities in coaching stock as appropriate.

Individual modifications to the basic schemes are described in the captions to the relevant photographs.

Inter City scheme 1

Full-length charcoal grey upper body half, white lower body half with broad red band. Charcoal grey front window frames. BR double arrow logo and Inter City in white within grey band. Loco number in white under nearside cab front windows. Yellow front end extended below cab side windows.

Class 43 had main body in charcoal grey with yellow lower half body and white band separating colours. Inter City scheme 1 grey, white and red applied from behind side ventilation grille to rear end of body. BR double arrow logo and Inter City 125 in white within grey band. Locomotive number in white within yellow band. Some locomotives also had number in white on front end.

Inter City scheme 2

Full-length charcoal grey upper body half, white lower body half with broad red band. Charcoal grey or yellow front window frames. Intercity in italic capital letters in white, sometimes plus swallow motif where ventilation grilles allowed space. Small black loco number at base of white area below nearside cab window.

(Note: Two Class 86s had upper body halves in dark chocolate for a period. A few Class 43s on Great Western lines had the red band replaced with one in claret. These variations were almost indistinguishable from the standard colours.)

Mainline

As Inter City schemes 1 and 2, but without any Inter City wording. Some locomotives had BR double arrow logos of varying sizes in white within the grey band; others had no identification whatsoever.

Provincial Sector

For Classes 142 and 143, lightish blue bodies with a broad dark blue band in the lower half with a thin white band between it and the base of the window frames. White BR double

North London Lines

Above: Provincial Sector No 143008 is parked at Kingmoor shed in April 1986, presumably having come from Bishop Auckland as the destination board reads. A Class 25 and Class 108 rest in the background.

arrow within the dark blue band. Full unit number in black on yellow front end.

Class 150 had pale blue upper body half, white lower half with broad dark blue band. BR double arrow in white within dark blue band at one end of unit. Full unit number in black on yellow front end.

Regional Railways
DMUs and EMUs: Darkish blue upper body half, white lower body half with pale blue band terminating in three thin black lines at each end. Regional Railways

wording and unit number in white within blue body half for Classes 101 and 153. BR double arrow logo and Sprinter wording with running man logo in black in lower part of white body half for Classes 150, 154, 155 and 156. Class 305 had no identification. Black front cab window frames.

Class 158 and some Class 156s had white with charcoal window frames. Stone colour bands above window frames and at bottom of body side. Charcoal and pale blue bands below windows with Express wording applied towards one end of body.

Locomotives: Darkish blue upper body half, white lower body half with pale blue band terminating in three thin black lines at each end. Regional Railways wording and loco number in white within blue body half.

Black front cab window frames. Abbreviated loco number in black on yellow front end.

London & South East
(*known as Jaffa Cake*)
Chocolate upper body half, dark stone lower body half with orange band separating them below window frames. White BR double arrow and coach number in white within stone band. Class 309 also had Essex Express wording in white. Black unit numbers on yellow front end.

Network South East scheme 1
Medium blue body with broad white band containing red stripe below, and grey band below this to base of body side. Bands and stripes swept upwards at end of body (to below white cab side windows for locomotives; to roof at end of body for MUs) with sharp angle at bend. White stripe along top of body side.

Locomotives: Loco number, BR double arrow logo and Network South East wording all in white within blue body area, but South East only in white outline. Yellow front panel brought round side of cab to meet up with grey band.

MUs: Very thin red stripe above white stripe above windows. BR double arrow logo in one of the bands behind side cab window,

Below: In NSE scheme 1 colours, No 50002 *Superb* slogs up the Lickey Incline past Vigo with a South West to North East inter-regional express in March 1987. At this time, the coaches are still in a variety of colours.

NSE three-colour strip logo or Network South East wording in blue within white band, all depending on class of unit. Yellow front end not extended around cab sides.

Network South East scheme 2

Locomotives: Medium blue body with broad white band containing red stripe below, and grey band below this to base of body side. Bands and stripes along full length of body. Yellow front end brought round front side very slightly to a very obtuse point lining up with bottom of blue body side. White band at top of body side between cabs. Loco number and NSE inscriptions in white as NSE scheme 1.

MUs: As NSE scheme 1, but angle at bend is rounded off and shade of blue is slightly darker. Note that Class 121 is treated as loco scheme 2.

Network South East scheme 3

Blue body with white surrounds and roof; red stripes below and above windows with broad red band angled by cab side windows. White spoilers. NSE three-colour strip logo and full unit number under cab front windows, except Class 442 where unit number is under cab side window.

Network South East variations

Class 319: In schemes 1 & 2, grey surrounds to cab, combined with the lower grey bodyside bands.

Class 419: Standard blue body with white, red and grey bands and stripes along full length of body, but without any inscriptions.

Class 456: Grey cab surrounds, roof and spoilers with black window frames.

Class 482 (Waterloo & City Line): White body and roof with blue doors, blue front end and blue body band. Broad grey band at base of body and around front end, separated from white areas by thin red stripe. Black window frames and front panels. Network South East and NSE three-colour logo between central sliding doors. White six-figure unit number was added in nearside black front panel.

Class 483 (Isle of Wight): White body with white band brought over top of cab windows. Light grey roof. Blue window frames with blue band above. Red body stripe separated from blue windows by white band, both red and white stripe and band angled up to front around cab side window and brought along length of body above blue band. NSE three-colour logo on front end. Three-figure unit number is shown twice on end.

Class 485/6 (Isle of Wight): Blue upper body, white central body and grey body base, with red stripe in lower part of white area. Three-colour NSE logo and Network South East wording in white area. Full-width black across front windows with white silhouette of Isle of Wight in centre with Ryde Rail wording below and NSE logo above. Six-figure unit number at top of yellow front. BR double arrow logo and Ryde Rail wording in white within blue area behind side cab window.

Class 487 (Waterloo & City Line): Blue upper body, white lower body and grey band at base of body with red stripe in lower part of white area. White cab front with blue connecting door with NSE three-colour logo at top of door. NSE logo and Network South East wording in white area between sliding doors. Two-figure unit number in blue within white area between cab and sliding doors. White BR double arrow logo in blue area behind cab.

(Note: Multiple-units in Jaffa Cake and NSE colours had full six-figure unit numbers on the front ends with the exception of Classes 415 to 457 inclusive. These units carried only the last four figures of the unit number on each side of the front end, apart from Class 442 which had the four-figure numbers under the side cab windows. Classes 483 and 487 are described above.)

ScotRail

Full-length charcoal grey upper body, white lower body half with broad light blue (Class 47/7) or red (Class 47/6) band. Charcoal grey front windows. BR double arrow logo and ScotRail wording in white within charcoal band. Loco number in white under cab side windows. Yellow front extended below cab side windows.

(Note: No 47706 operated for several months without identification logos.)

Parcels

Black band along upper part of body, extending around front windows. Red lower body side. Black cab doors. Loco number in white under nearside cab windows. Brass BR double arrow logo under offside cab windows.

Rail Express Systems

Red body with black band in top part along three-quarters of body length, with shaped downwards extension at non-cab end. Two pairs of light blue rectangles in two different lengths superimposed over and alongside this extension. Black cab window frames and cab doors. White loco number under nearside cab windows. Brass BR double arrow logo fitted to some engines.

Royal Mail

Red body with two full-length yellow stripes at lower part of body side. Large doors highlighted with diagonal yellow strips across them. Crown surmounting ER cipher with Royal Mail wording alongside, and Royal Mail Letters in yellow above lower stripes. White BR double arrow logo under nearside cab windows.

Network North West

White body with blue window frames. Stripe in green along three-quarters of body centre with red stripes at each end separated by thin white stripe from green band. NNW logo in red and blue behind driver's cab door, and BR double arrow logo in red below cab side window, both logos in white area below red stripe. Black unit number on front end.

Stansted Express

Very pale grey upper body and white lower body with light grey roof. Broad green band in top part of white area with thin black stripe below separated from green band by white stripe. Stansted Express wording in black letters occupies space between end of green band and front of unit. Black front windows and number on front end.

Gatwick Express

Black top half of body, white bottom half with thin claret stripe along length of body in white area. Grey Gatwick Express wording and double flash logo in black area. Loco has orange OHE warning stripe at cantrail level; coaches have white stripe at this level. Driving luggage van has black front windows with two white four-figure unit numbers, some units also having the double flash logo between the unit numbers.

Thameslink scheme 1

Light grey body with blue Thameslink wording under windows at left-hand end of each coach. Two sets of blue and red shapes on each coach side. Dark grey roof. Black unit number on front end. Red line under cantrail.

Thameslink scheme 2

Black body with orange band in lower body side formed into a point at the front end and separated by white stripes from the black area. The white stripes are brought round the front end under the black area which is also brought round under the yellow front end. A white stripe at cantrail level is formed into a triangle at the front end where the black area is blended into the front end. Thameslink wording in black within orange band. Black unit number on front end. Dark blue front spoiler.

Eurostar
White body with yellow band at base of body tapered into end of front spoiler. Yellow front end is swept along each side of black front window and tapered off above cab side door. Yellow 'eurostar' wording and black three-strip logo at side of cab with black four-figure unit number.

Special colour schemes
(*stock in regular service*)
Class 08 No 08833: Great Eastern Railway blue with red lining. BR lion crest, Stratford depot cockney sparrow logo. White lettering including Liverpool Street Pilot in italic script, engine number, class, shed allocation and painting details all in white. Red coupling rods. White cab roof.

Class 08 No 08869: Dark green with white roof and yellow coupling rods. Yellow-backed nameplate with polished letters, *The Canary*. Yellow canary logo on lighter green circle. White number.

Class 33 No 33008: This locomotive went through three reincarnations from silver-roofed BR blue to reach its final original BR green with yellow front panel. The first version featured a full yellow front end with green body, with white bodyside band; the second version had white window frames and roof, white bodyside band with white

BR double arrow logos under each cab side window and white number behind nearside cab door.

Class 47 Nos 47475: Provincial Services livery. Blue body with white lower body side containing light blue band. Yellow front swept round cab sides. Black window frames. Black number at base of yellow swept nearside. Yellow cab roof.

Class 47 No 47484/500/628 (and freight sector No 47079): Great Western Railway green with body panel lined out in black and orange. Brass BR double arrow logo on offside cab. Cast number on nearside cab and cast name in GW style lettering with GWR crests below. Green cab roof.

Class 47 No 47522: Apple-type green with two thin white stripes with black stripe between at base of body. Yellow front end swept round cab sides. Silver roof. Large white number and BR double arrow logo at opposite ends of body panel. Black-backed nameplate. Stratford depot cockney sparrow logo. (Note: This loco originally carried the word 'Parcels' alongside the BR logo.)

Class 47 No 97561 (later 47561): Crimson Lake body with thin yellow stripe at top and bottom of body. Yellow front end swept round cab sides. Black window frames.

Above: A depot pet was Norwich's No 08869 *The Canary,* which served as the station pilot for that city's terminus. The engine waits for business in June 1987.

Class 50 No D400 (originally 50050 in NSE colours): BR blue with D400 and BR double arrow logo in white under each cab side. Later fitted with small red oval panel in centre of bodyside to record restoration to this colour through contributions initiated by Rail magazine.

Class 50 No 50007: Great Western Railway green with single back stripe lined out in orange in lower part of body side. Yellow side cab windows. Number plate and nameplate in GW style lettering. Brass BR logo on offside cab side.

Class 73 No 73101: Cream and umber Pullman style. Cream upper body, umber lower body, cantrail band, cab front window and cab sides. Umber areas lined out in thin gold stripes, and gold number under nearside cab windows. Pullman wording in gold with red shading in cantrail band. White roof. Nameplate in cream body area, originally named *Brighton Evening Argus*, later *The Royal Alex*.

Above: No 87006 *City of Glasgow* in its unique experimental IC colour scheme brings an up express of Mark 1, 2 & 3 stock past Ledburn Junction on a misty autumn day in October 1984.

Class 87 No 87006: Charcoal grey body with white large logo and number. Yellow cab roof. (Note: This experimental IC livery was replaced before sectorisation, but is included since InterCity itself preceded the 1986 sector introductions.)

Class 117 set B430: Great Western Railway chocolate and cream with silver roof and headcode panel. Black set number on front end.

Class 142: Off-white body with broad chocolate band along centre of body below windows, containing white BR double arrow logo. Black front windows and headcode panel. Black unit number on front end.

Class 151: Light stone body with light blue lower body band above which is thin white stripe and slightly wider navy blue stripe; these bands and stripes swept up to cantrail level behind wrap-round yellow cab sides. Black front window frames. Black unit number in yellow front end, black coach number and white BR double arrow logo in light blue band.

Class 205 No 205029: Plain green with white numbers for First Class on doors and white coach numbers. Black unit number at top of yellow front end.

Class 321 No 321334: Dutch NS livery with blue windows and yellow bodies. Black front cab windows and spoiler. Black NS logo and coach numbers in yellow area. Black unit number above coupling.

Note 1: A number of older locomotives and multiple-units, mainly withdrawn, were painted in varieties of green liveries. These include the 2BIL/4SUB EMUs, Class 40 D200, Class 55 D9000, Class 71 E5001, Class 415 5001 etc, but although they operated during the period under review, since they were not used in regular service, for space reasons they have had to be omitted.

Note 2: In the earlier days of sectorisation, multiple-units in the Network South East area which had not been repainted into that sector's colours and were still in the previous BR blue and grey scheme had small three-colour NSE logos either on the front end or on body sides according to class. Pictures of these are not included so that space can be devoted to showing the range of sectorised colour schemes.

Strathclyde PTE
Orange body with black window frames. Strathclyde Transport wording and BR double arrow logo in black outlined in white on lower half of body. Black unit number on front end.

Tyne & Wear PTE
White window frames and band, under which a blue band above a yellow lower body side. Thin yellow stripe above windows. Black cab windows and headcode panel. Regional Railways wording in black within yellow body area. Black unit number on front end.

West Yorkshire PTE scheme 1
Class 141 only. White body and roof with broad green band along body side under windows. White front cab windows. MetroTrain wording and logo in white in green band. Black headcode panel. Black unit number on front end.

West Yorkshire PTE scheme 2
Red body side with broad white band under windows and thin yellow stripe just above base of body. Black front cab windows on DMUs, not on EMUs. Red MetroTrain wording with M in red circle logo and BR double arrow logo in white band. Black unit number on front end.

South Yorkshire PTE
Cream upper body with chocolate band at base of body and along cantrail, brought round cab door. South Yorkshire Transport wording and SYT logo next to cab door in cream area, together with unit coach number.

Greater Manchester PTE scheme 1
Class 142 only. Orange body with broad white band above windows. White M logo and white BR double arrow logo in black square by nearside door; white BR logo by offside front door. Black headcode panel. Black unit number on front end.

Greater Manchester PTE scheme 2
Orange body with chocolate colour window frames outlined in white. White BR double arrow logo in orange body area, and also M logo with Class 304. Black unit number on front end, except Class 304 which has black coach number.

Greater Manchester PTE scheme 3
White upper body, black lower body with red stripe between. Black front cab windows. White Regional Railways wording in black body area at nearside front. Black unit number on front end.

Merseyrail PTE scheme 1
Multiple-units: White upper body and yellow lower body separated by grey and black bands. Yellow stripe above white band. Yellow M logo in black circle in yellow square within white band. Regional Railways wording in black in yellow band. Black unit number on front end.

Merseyrail PTE scheme 2
Class 73: Yellow body with broad black band at base. Yellow M logo in black circle, black Regional Railways wording and loco number all in yellow area.

West Midlands PTE scheme 1
Canary yellow body including front end, with blue window frames. Black front cab windows and headcode panel. White WM logo and BR double arrow logo each side of driver's cab door. Black unit number on front end.

West Midlands PTE scheme 2
Blue body with light stone lower body separated by blue and stone stripes. West Midlands logo in blue and red on white background in nearside stone area behind driver's cab door. Black front cab window and headcode panel and black unit number on front end.

West Midlands PTE scheme 3
Green upper body and white lower body with broad blue band between and very thin yellow stripe in white stripe above blue band. White band above green body area. Green WM logo in yellow square by doors in green area. Black front cab windows and black unit number on front end.

West Midlands PTE scheme 4
Unit T133 only. Three-tone blue body. Centre blue band contains Midline wording in blue and red in white rectangle, white WM logo and BR double arrow logo each side of rectangle on nearside front end, and coach number in white at other end. Yellow front ends brought round to side cab window with diagonal ends. Unit, but not class, number in black on unit ends.

Below: No 73205 *London Chamber of Commerce* is permanently allocated and coupled to No 83301 and the RTC-liveried 4TC set for the Eurostar bogie-testing programme. It speeds through Winchfield in September 1990 on its return trip from Eastleigh to Stewarts Lane, making a very colourful change from the normal traffic.

Transition from BR Blue

Below: Class 08 No 08717 shunts the stock off the sleeper from Euston, whilst Large Logo 47563, ScotRail No 47541 and another 47 are stabled in front of Inverness shed. Another Class 47 is ready to depart from the station with an express, and a Class 08 is parked with a variety of vans. A fifth 47 sits in the stabling sidings. This view was taken from the top of the Blue Circle silos in May 1987.

Left: One of Stratford's special Class 47s with a silver roof heads a set of mixed Inter City and blue and grey coaches forming a Norwich to Liverpool Street express near Needham Market when electrification only went as far as Stowmarket, in September 1985.

Right: Class 419 luggage van No 68004 contrasts with a London & South East Class 411 set as it brings its boat train from Dover Western Docks into Platform 2 at London Victoria in September 1985.

Below: The shunters have done a good job making up the stock in a regular format for this Waterloo to Exeter express seen here near Barford St Martin. The date is October 1986 and the locomotive is No 50036 *Victorious* which, in my opinion, carries the best livery in which this class was ever seen.

Above: A mixture of Strathclyde PTE and BR colours is seen on Class 107 445, approaching Glasgow Central with its train from Largs in March 1987.

Below: A 'Flying Banana' power car with Inter City stock at Paddington. No 43139 has just arrived with an express from Swansea in September 1985.

Right: Class 08 No 08873 shows off its clean colours at the open day at Bounds Green in May 1987. Note the Stratford cockney sparrow shed logo, yellow coupling rods and cab roof, and white handrails and piping. A mystery hand holds the window down!

Below: Class 09 No 09012 *Dick Hardy*, shunts the down yard at Woking in May 1989. The cast nameplate and red coupling rods give it a touch of elegance.

Above: Class 31 No 31422 shows off its Mainline colours as it ambles along the up main line at Colton Junction in July 1991, BR logo at one end, white number at the other.

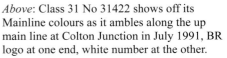

Left: Class 33 No 33115 was converted and introduced into service in May 1990 for testing the bogie design and current collection for the Eurostars. It worked in between Class 73 No 73205 and a 4TC set (later increased to a 6TC). It was renumbered No 83301 and painted in Mainline livery with the inscription 'Test Vehicle for International Services', and is seen here near Elvetham in July 1992. The unique bogie design can be seen quite clearly.

Left: No 37426 in Mainline livery enters Preston station with a Manchester Victoria to Blackpool train in July 1991, with coaching stock in Regional Railways colours. A Class 87 lurks in the distance.

Right: Another Mainline Class 37, this time No 37409 *Loch Awe*, is leaving Fort William on its way south with the 'Royal Scotsman' tour train in June 1991. Note the headboard of classic design and abbreviated number under the headlamp.

Right: Whilst the Class 91s were being tested and before Mark 4 DVTs were introduced, Class 43 power cars were used as rear end driving vehicles. They were fitted with conventional buffers and were normally in standard InterCity livery. However, this example, No 43014, appeared in this variation of a full yellow end with a white band around the front end, and black number under the front window. It trails a test train which is entering Doncaster in August 1988. See the front of the train under Class 91.

Below: Another buffer-fitted Class 43 displays the final version of InterCity as it heads this HST, passing Huntingdon with a Leeds to King's Cross express in May 1989. The A14 trunk road dominates the background.

Left: Inter City No 47471 *Norman Tunna* GC smokes well as it leaves Ryecroft Junction behind to make its way along the Sutton Park line in August 1989 with a track assessment train.

Below: HM The Queen is on her way from Windsor to Southampton in July 1993 and catches me by surprise! No 47835 *Windsor Castle* is resplendent, as are the crew with smart ties (and presumably well-polished boots), as it heads past Potbridge with a 5-coach Royal trainset.

Above: Windsor & Eton Riverside rarely sees locomotives within its walls, but on this occasion No 47567 *Red Star* is seen whilst running round empty stock to go to Hollinwood. The loco is in Mainline colours and the 'Red Star' emblem relating to Post Office parcels services can be seen above the nameplate. And what a very nice clean station.

Below: The WCML is closed at Stonebridge Park for widening of the North Circular Road so Liverpool expresses are diverted to St Pancras. At Souldrop No 47973 *Derby Evening Telegraph* pilots No 90001 *BBC Midlands Today* down Sharnbrook bank in October 1991.

Above: Immaculate Mainline No 47566 shows up the grubby stock of the Gillingham to Preston parcels train as it accelerates the train away from Guildford in May 1989. NSE Classes 455, 423 and 117 lurk at the platforms.

Below: No 73123 *Gatwick Express* is in a preliminary version of InterCity livery as it leaves Gatwick Airport station for Victoria in May 1984. The number in the upper half of the body, full wrap round yellow ends and silver roof are unique. Note the 'Gatwick Express' branding on the coaching stock.

Right: Passenger locomotives did not always work passenger or parcels trains. No 73102 *Airtour Suisse* was very much a dedicated Gatwick Express engine, but that did not stop it being summoned to take the Rugby Cement empties from Bevois Park to Halling one Saturday in July 1985. It is seen here climbing up to Battledown flyover.

Below: During 1987/88 when the Class 442s were being built, the motors from 4REP Class 432s were used in the new trains and 4REP power cars were gradually withdrawn. During this period, Class 73s were seconded to mainline services to Poole and Weymouth, sometimes hauling 4TC sets, but in some cases replacing a 4REP power car at one end of a set, leaving the other power car in situ (the 3REP remaining was renumbered into a Class 4329xx series). This view, taken above the west end of Southampton tunnel, shows Mainline-liveried No 73126 with a 3REP and 4TC set leaving Southampton Central on its way from Weymouth to Waterloo in April 1988. Note the maritime flags on the footbridge.

Above: The later versions of InterCity and mainline liveries did not have a wrap-round yellow end. This is clearly seen on No 73138 *Post Haste* which is shunting the yard at Chichester in the shadow of the cathedral in April 1989. Note the very small number and also the close-up of the nameplate on page 94.

Left: A very clean No 73202 *Royal Observer Corps* is decked out in full InterCity colours as it tows NSE-liveried Class 421 No 1314 past Raynes Park, probably going to the depot at Wimbledon. Note the blue-backed nameplate with crest above, and the 73A shed badge above the headlight. The date is March 1993.

Above: One Class 82 and one Class 83 were retained after the withdrawal of their sisters for working empty stock in and out of Euston. They were painted into Mainline livery but without BR logos. No 83012 is seen here on display amidst the junk at the Basford Hall open day in August 1995, after being preserved at Barrow Hill.

Right: In the days when electrification went only as far as Cambridge, No 86214 *Sanspareil* arrives with an express from Liverpool Street to King's Lynn at 11:57. Will the engine change be quick enough for it to leave on time? The loco is in standard Inter City scheme 1 colours, with blue and grey coaching stock.

Right: Trainspotters record the locomotive destroyed in the Colwich accident, No 86429 *The Times,* which is seen at Euston ready to back off the station in September 1985. A close-up of the nameplate is shown on page 94.

Above: A glinty shot of a marvellous selection of mail and parcels vans heading north past Hatch End in February 1990. In Inter City scheme 2 colours, No 86234 *J. B. Priestley O.M.* does the honours.

Below: A pair of InterCity 86s are in charge of this colourful southbound Freightliner at Headstone Lane in May 1990. The lead loco is No 86430 *Scottish National Orchestra*, and No 86439 trails. Both engines are in scheme 2 livery.

Right: In the early days of InterCity, some locomotives did not carry the brand name and had the BR logo painted in black on the offside cab side, as seen here on No 87018 *Lord Nelson* as it comes to a stop at Oxenholme in April 1985 with a Glasgow to Euston express.

Left: *Lord Nelson* is seen again, by this time in the Inter City scheme 2 colours, no wrap-round yellow end, InterCity in italic letters and a tiny number. The occasion is the rather cramped open day at Colchester in May 1988 and what the man on top of the 'Deltic' is about to do gives rise to speculation!

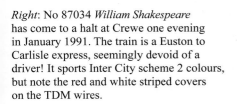

Right: No 87034 *William Shakespeare* has come to a halt at Crewe one evening in January 1991. The train is a Euston to Carlisle express, seemingly devoid of a driver! It sports Inter City scheme 2 colours, but note the red and white striped covers on the TDM wires.

Above: The unique Class 89, No 89001, stands alongside Bounds Green shed in November 1988. It is technically in Mainline livery, although in practice always worked InterCity services. The number is also carried under the front window in white.

Left: No 89001 is seen here speeding through Hatfield in July 1988 on the Mallard Anniversary special from King's Cross to Doncaster. The whole train gleams, with white wheel rims throughout. Highly polished buffers and the front number can be seen, although slightly blurred since the train was going faster than my shutter speed had anticipated.

Above: This view of No 90019 has been chosen to show the white roof and black well for the electrics. The train is a Glasgow to Plymouth express, seen near Coseley in the West Midlands in August 1989. Putting the restaurant car next to the engine is a bit hard for people at the back of the train. The mast projecting from the engine is as worthy as a pole from the chimney of a steam loco!

Below: Floriston has been a favourite break point for me on my way to Scotland over the years, and on this occasion No 90018 was heading south with a Glasgow to Birmingham express. Taken with permission from trackside staff in June 1991.

Above: After a shower, the winter sun lights up No 90029 in Mainline livery at Crewe with an unidentified train in February 1990. Again the restaurant car is next to the engine. Note the metal BR logo on the cab side.

Below: Class 91 No 91004 arrives at Doncaster in August 1988 with a test train comprising an RTC test car, five sleeping cars and the Class 43 No 43014 illustrated on page 19. Note the swallow emblem in addition to the Intercity italics.

Above: Apart from when they were built and first used Crewe electric depot for major overhauls, the Class 91s hardly strayed from the East Coast Main Line, except in late June 1993 when No 91001 *Swallow* undertook a number of demonstration runs on the West Coast Main Line. This rare shot shows it on the return run to Glasgow at Hatch End, still with Mark 3 stock at that time.

Below: A non-standard carrier of the InterCity-style livery was this ex-Class 25, No 97251 also known as Ethel 2, parked here at Upperby in February 1988. The black front window framing is non-standard, as is the total lack of ownership identification.

Above: One Class 08 painted in Provincial Sector colours was No 08761 seen here with its model-railway-sized train at Thornton Junction in May 1991. One hopes the black oil spill did not cover the driver's front window.

Below: A fully matched trainset headed by No 31465, labelled for Regional Railways, is entering Liverpool Lime Street in September 1993, with a train from Blackpool. Marker lights in the headcode panel are well lit!

Right: Definitely not a normal duty for a Regional Railways Class 31 is shown in this view of a southbound ballast train at Headstone Lane in April 1997, i.e. post-privatisation. No 31465 is seen again leading two-tone grey No 37888.

Right: In May 1994, Regional Railways No 37418 *East Lancashire Railway* leads a Manchester to Holyhead train past the signalbox at Mold Junction (or what used to be the junction). The first coach is in ex-NSE livery without the red stripe.

Below: Class 101 No 101656, labelled for Regional Railways, passes plinthed Class 08 D3167 as it enters Lincoln station with a train from Gainsborough in March 1992. Not only have the semaphore signals gone, so has the 08.

Left: No 122112 looks very smart as with its colleague in blue and grey it makes a smoky, leisurely start at Exeter St Davids with a service to Exmouth in January 1992.

Right: During a lunchbreak from work in Perth, the last thing you would expect to see at Stanley Junction is a Provincial Sector 142 and a West Yorkshire PTE 141. But just south of the junction in April 1991, No 142076 leads No 141108 from Inverness to heaven knows where, and for what purpose had they been there?

Left: In more normal territory, No 142080 ambles away from Ulceby station on its way from Barton-on-Humber to Cleethorpes in March 1992. Colours are standard Provincial Sector.

Right: The two prototype Class 150s were done out in a different scheme to that of the main production units which are seen in the following picture. In a light grey scheme with dark blue windows, light blue stripe and black front window frames, No 150002 leaves Derby for Matlock on a cold and miserable morning in March 1986.

Below: No 150101 is seen at Chesterfield in October 1985 on its delivery trip from York to Derby. Everything is spotless including the yellow battery box and silver exhaust piping.

Above: A pair of Class 150s, No 150149 leading, enter Llandudno Junction with an unidentified working in June 1987. The first unit is in the original Provincial Sector scheme, the trailing unit in the later scheme with Sprinter logos, but not Regional Railways wording.

Below: No 150271 shows off its Sprinter logos on the later Provincial scheme as it clears the semaphores at the exit of Yeovil Pen Mill. The date is April 1992, and the train is travelling from Bristol Temple Meads to Weymouth.

Above: An Edinburgh to Kirkcaldy train is in the hands of Class 150 No 150255, seen between North Queensferry and Inverkeithing in April 1991. By this date many units will have been labelled for Regional Railways, but neither this nor the train in the preceding picture has been so enhanced.

Below: This class 150, No 150224, looks strange without full yellow panelling, and whilst clean looks all the better. How long it remained like this is unknown, but it is seen here in March 1987 stabled at York. In all other respects it is in later Provincial colours.

Above: Class 153s were starting to take over services on the Exmouth branch when this shot was taken in March 1992. No 153318 had just left Topsham on its way to Exmouth from Exeter St Davids. Regional Railways labels had been applied this time.

Left: A pair of Class 155s are seen at Salisbury on a dull day in July 1991. No 155327 is stabled in the bay platform, whilst No 155301 enters the station with a Portsmouth Harbour to Cardiff service. Both units are in later Provincial Sector colours, but No 155301 is of particular interest since it carries a Leyland logo on the front in recognition of the fact that this company built the bodies.

Left: Another shot of a Class 155, taken at Liskeard in February 1991 to show the variety of signals. No 155330 leaves with a service from Penzance to Bristol.

Above: In conjunction with the open day held at Colchester in May 1988, Class 156 No 156408 is seen outside the shed ready to work a train to Clacton. Note the standard scheme 2 Provincial Sector colours, with Sprinter and BR logos clearly visible.

Right: A post-privatisation picture showing one of the Class 156s which were painted in the scheme similar to that of the Class 158s. No 156401, carrying a Central Trains label, passes the flyover at Bishton on a Cardiff to Nottingham working in July 1998.

Above: A dark sky brings out the colours of this Class 158 at Helpston in March 1993. No 158782 makes its way from Liverpool to Stansted Airport, showing off the colour scheme that, apart from the few Class 156s as seen before, was restricted to this class.

Left: No 158785 leaves the tunnel by Frodsham station on its way from Manchester to Llandudno in April 1994.

Left: One of the less common classes of the Provincial/Regional Railways was the Class 305 EMU. This example, No 305504, is waiting to leave Manchester Piccadilly for Hazel Grove in May 1992. The unit does not even carry a BR logo, let alone anything else.

Above: Jaffa Cake colours are seen on No 309613 arriving at Manningtree in July 1986 with a Harwich to Liverpool Street train. Essex Express, BR logo, coach number and number 1 for First Class accomodation show up nicely in the stone band. The OHE label in the offside window seems somewhat misplaced.

Right: Class 411 4CEP 1600 speeds away from Polhill tunnel with a Charing Cross to Hastings express in July 1986. Under the offside cab window is a plate stating 'Ride The 1066 Electrics' to commemorate the electrification of the Hastings line.

Above: Only the Southern Region could put together a combination such as this. A pair of Class 419 motor luggage vans, No 9007 leading, are followed by a Class 489 Gatwick Express driving van and a Class 438 4TC set. The Southern Electric Group special is on the approach to Guildford from Woking in May 1988.

Below: The least common of the Jaffa Cake-coloured units was the Class 421 4CIG sets. No 1701 leads No 1706 in bright sunshine at Gatwick Airport on its way from Victoria to Brighton in March 1986.

Right: The only Class 03 to appear in Network South East colours was one of the two of this class stationed on the Isle of Wight. No 03179 is seen parked in the bay platform at Sandown in January 1990, looking very much like a Ryde shed pet.

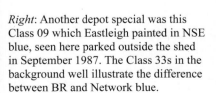

Left: Slade Green tarted up a Class 08 in Network colours and named it after the TV character 'Ivor the Engine'. It is seen at the Woking open day in May 1988 complete with details on the buffer beam, shaded gold name, NSE and BR logos, red coupling rods and yellow axle ends etc. Note the number – 97800.

Right: Another depot special was this Class 09 which Eastleigh painted in NSE blue, seen here parked outside the shed in September 1987. The Class 33s in the background well illustrate the difference between BR and Network blue.

Above: The harvest is in during August 1995, as we see NSE scheme 2-liveried No 47715 Haymarket bring a full set of RES parcels vans past Colton Junction with a Low Fell to Plymouth service, the type of train no longer seen on the British rail system.

Below: One of the first locomotives to receive NSE colours was No 47573 *The Evening Standard*, which is seen here waiting to leave King's Lynn with an express for Liverpool Street in August 1986. The first version of NSE loco colours is seen clearly, and contrasts with the BR blue and grey stock. Note the non-standard lettering on the name plate.

Above: The evening sun catches the train and highlights the exhaust from No 47707 *Holyrood* as it cimbs Honiton bank near Watchcombe in August 1991. The loco, in the second NSE loco colours, is working a Waterloo to Exeter service. A lovely way to spend an evening!

Below: A pair of Class 47s is rather excessive for the four vans of the Redhill to Bristol morning empties. NSE scheme 2 No 47521 pilots InterCity No 47814 past the foot crossing between Sandhurst and Crowthorne in July 1993. Note the dip under the overbridge which was put in when the line was being upgraded to take freight from the Channel Tunnel to the Midlands and north of England, which of course never materialised.

Above: Class 50 No 50032 *Courageous* is climbing away from Gillingham (Dorset) with a Waterloo to Exeter express in April 1988. The engine is in NSE scheme 1 loco colours, but note the blue-backed nameplate and the NSE logo on the route indicator panel.

Below: A powerful combination on an Exeter to Waterloo train at Potbridge in January 1992. No 50030 *Repulse* leads No 47716 *Duke of Edinburgh's Award*, but note the lighter shade of NSE scheme 2 blue on the Class 50 compared with the 47 and the rest of the train. This shade was that used for NSE scheme 1 and somehow was used for a scheme 2 loco.

Right: On a perfectly lit morning in August 1991, No 50037 *Illustrious* approaches Pinhoe with a Waterloo to Exeter express, marred only by one blue and grey coach. The NSE scheme 2 locomotive carries a West of England NSE logo below the nameplate. For a short period, this engine was painted in all-over dark blue with silver roof.

Right: One more shot of an NSE Class 50 – and why not? They were a favourite class. In this example, No 50033 is in charge of a Paddington to Oxford service at West Ealing in February 1990. Note how the position of the nameplate enables it to read '*Glorious Network South East*'! And could you get a much cleaner loco?

Below: Well, you could get a cleaner loco than No 50033 above, because the only blemishes on No 73129 *City of Winchester* are the grease spots in the centre of the buffers. Everthing sparkles, including the nameplate and crest, as it sits in the stabling sidings alongside the Tonbridge line at Redhill in August 1992.

Above: No 73136 *Kent Youth Music* in NSE scheme 2 colours is propelling the two Class 438 4TC sets which were restored to original BR blue for coaching stock. The train is a special from Poole to Waterloo, the date is November 1992, and the location Winchfield.

Left: Two Class 73s were painted in shades of NSE blue. No 73004 *The Bluebell Railway* is stabled at Waterloo in May 1989. It has a blue body extending round the cab widows, yellow cab roofs, but silver main body roof, and a black number, white BR logo and red nameplate.

Below: In September 1988, a special was run from the Mid Hants Railway to Waterloo and back. In charge was No 73005 *Mid Hants/ Watercress Line*, in a lighter shade of NSE blue than No 73004. The blue sides extended along the full length of the body, as did the silver roof, and the cab front window frames were black. With white numbers, BR logo and red nameplate, the train with its 'Watercress Belle' headboard is seen near Bentley on the return trip.

Above: Only one Class 86 was painted in NSE colours, namely No 86401, which was done up in conjunction with the electrification from Liverpool Street to Cambridge. Subsequently named *Northampton Town*, it is seen here at Watford Junction in February 1989 in scheme 1 NSE colours; it never received the later scheme.

Right: Class 101 L837 is passing Betchworth in April 1991 with a Reading to Gatwick Airport service. The unit is in scheme 2 NSE colours with the rounded red stripe angle under the cab door. Note the name *Heidi* under the NSE logo on the front end, an embellishment applied by Reading depot to a few of this class. The CCTV at the crossing contrasts with the gas lamps on the station.

Left: A very clean Class 104 waits at Gospel Oak before departure for Barking in May 1989. Set number L703 is in the scheme 2 version.

Below: Early in NSE days, a Class 115 is waiting to leave Aylesbury for Marylebone. Note the red BR logo and Chiltern Line wording in red within the white band behind the cab window. In June 1986, only NSE scheme 1 with the sharp-angled band corner applied. The flowerbed adds to the scene, but some extra blue flowers would have made a better match!

Right: A very clean bubble car is Class 121 L129 on a Bedford to Bletchley stopping service approaching Forders Siding in May 1995. Note the silvered exhaust pipes and buffers, and the Bedford-Bletchley NSE logo.

Below: The current stock on the LSWR line to Exeter is seen here in its early days as No 159004 passes Byfleet & New Haw on a driver training run in March 1993. It sports standard NSE scheme 3 livery with the white roof and front spoiler.

Above: On a test trip from where it was built – York – No 165108 returns to the BR workshops as it passes Dringhouses in May 1992. The phase 3 scheme shows up well in the afternoon sun, with the white roof, spoiler and base band, which replaces the grey of schemes 1 and 2.

Below: A Hampshire unit rounds the bend at Portcreek Junction in May 1989, on its way from Salisbury to Portsmouth Harbour. No 205030 carries scheme 2 colours with a very white toilet window, and the correct 87 headcode.

BR PASSENGER SECTORS IN COLOUR

Right: In May 1992, the Oxted Thumpers were not common on the Reading to Basingstoke line, but here is No 207010 arriving at Bramley with such a service in May 1992. Scheme 2 colours, but note the Oxted line NSE logo in the middle of the body, and the unit number over each front window instead of above the headcode panel as on No 205030 opposite.

Below: Passing Caledonian Road in February 1993 is No 302998 with an unidentified special working. It carries scheme 2 colours, with the class and unit numbers in different case size on the front end, and an unidentified NSE logo on the bodyside by the guard's compartment.

Left: No 309601 has arrived at Liverpool Street in October 1988 with a service from Clacton. It is in NSE scheme 1 colours, with a typically grubby front end which affected this class. Note the white BR logo and a shed code label in the grey band, presumably one for Clacton depot.

Below: A post-privatisation shot, but who can tell? No 312095, in standard scheme 2 NSE colours with black front window frames, slowly heads into Fenchurch Street with a service from Leigh-on-Sea as seen from the DLR station at Tower Gateway in March 1997.

Left: No 313032 zooms past Welwyn North and enters the South tunnel in May 1989. It is an empty stock working, so whence has it come (Moorgate?) and whither does it go? No 313018 is the leading unit and both are in scheme 2 NSE colours, with the large unit numbers applied to this class.

Right: For a short period in 1987, some Class 313s and 315s omitted the black upper front end panels seen in the previous picture, giving a somewhat unfamiliar appearance. For what reason this was done I have no idea, but illustrating this variation is No 313003 leaving Hatch End on its way from Euston to Watford Junction in September of that year. In all other respects it carries NSE scheme 1 with the sharp angles.

Below: Standard Thameslink fare at Bedford in May 1988, where No 319009 is seen just after arriving, but not from Luton! The different treatment of the grey area at the front end from other classes is clearly seen. It is in NSE scheme 1 colours and carries Thameslink logos by the sliding doors.

Left: The NSE scheme 3 is lit up by the early evening sun which shows No 319179 making its way from Luton to Gatwick Airport in August 1991. The location is Salfords. This scheme was introduced on the second batch of Class 319s and is notably different from the colours of the original units as seen before. Note the grey roof which can be seen only from above.

Below: The Class 321s were introduced in scheme 3 NSE colours, as seen here on No 321401, heading along the down main line at South Kenton in August 1993 on a service from Euston to Northampton. The fairly Art Deco design of the waiting room and offices can be seen. Is the train on time at 13:35?

Above: The now abandoned station at Dover Western Docks was still accommodating trains in March 1992, when this Class 411 4CEP No 1542 had arrived from Victoria. Although it is not possible to distinguish in which NSE scheme the train is painted, the view showing the station details is worth reproduction.

Right: The 4CAP units were formed from pairs of Class 414 2HAPs semi-permanently coupled together and originally destined for South Coast Coastway services. However, their range extended into the South Eastern lines, and NSE scheme 2 Class 413 No 3201 is seen in January 1992, passing Wandsworth Road with a train for Victoria.

Right: On summer Saturdays in 1990, at least one Bournemouth to Waterloo semi-fast was made up of Class 414 2HAP units instead of normal corridor stock. Four such units, headed by No 4311 in NSE scheme 2 livery, speed through Beaulieu Road in August of that year. Note the unit numbers over each front window, and the inverted black triangle which indicates to station staff at which end is the luggage compartment. The train also carries an NSE logo which cannot be identified.

Above: The Class 415s were seen throughout the Southern suburban lines until replaced by Class 455s and 465s. Unit 5403, in NSE scheme 2 (modellers please note the limited graffiti), leaves Stone Crossing on its way from London Bridge to Gravesend in July 1993. The numbers over each front window indicate that this a refurbished unit. The lady in red keeps the staff occupied at this delightful example of a station building.

Below: A busy scene at St Mary Cray Junction in March 1990: a Class 419 motor luggage van in NSE colours, trailing a Jaffa Cake-liveried Class 411 4CEP working a Victoria to Dover Wetsern Docks service, meets another 4CEP approaching with a Maidstone East to Victoria train. The MLVs colours did not vary with scheme changes.

Right: 4CIG Class 421 No 1315 was fitted with a headlight and extra marker lights on the front end which did provide better illumination than just the light from the headcode. In NSE scheme 2 colours, this unit is working a Southampton to Waterloo semi-fast service as it stops at Micheldever in September 1990.

Middle: A few Central section units were turned out with black upper half front ends as seen here on Class 421 No 1860 working a Bournemouth service in March 1998, a post-privatisation shot. Note the white front numbers. The location is Mount Pleasant, Southampton.

Below: In the late 1980s, the authorities decided to move the unit numbers of Class 421s and 423s from above the cab windows to below them, where the position of the handrails made them more difficult to see. Fortunately they were restored to their original positions, but whilst in the temporary version the units looked as if they had lost their eyebrows! Showing this version, Class 423 4VEP No 3437 approaches Bosham station with a Portsmouth Harbour to Brighton service in April 1989, leaving behind the upper quadrant signal and passing the NSE-coloured signalbox.

Left: Probably the rarest Southern Region EMUs were the Class 431s, of which there were two types. Units 1901/2 were virtually 4REPs without a buffet car, but units 1903-6 were 6-coach sets made up from various combinations of 4REP and 4TC sets. Unit 1903 is working a Portsmouth Harbour to Waterloo train past Potbridge in August 1991. Note the ex-4TC driving trailers fitted with collector shoes, and the de-cabbed 4REP powered driving coach third in the set.

Below: The Class 442 5WES units always caused unit number identification problems, since unlike all the other Southern Region units, they never carried their unit numbers on the cab ends but in the white stripe behind the cab, as can be seen here. Two unidentified Class 442s speed through Winchfield in February 1991 on their way to Waterloo from Poole. That damned yellow bin was always in the way!

Left: A close-up of an original Class 442 buffet car at Eastleigh in September 1988. The doors are labelled 'Not for Public Use', the white stripe carries the coach number and Buffet wording, and there is a Wessex Electrics NSE logo visible.

Right: I make no excuse for showing other shots at Potbridge if it illustrates a particular unit better than my other shots. The grey front end, roof and lower body band show up clearly on unit 456005 which is on commissioning runs between Basingstoke and Woking in March 1991. Note the four South Central NSE logos by the sliding doors, and the black front window frames, NSE striped logo and two white unit numbers in full on the grey spoiler.

Right: Looking very much like a Class 455, this unit, Class 457 No 7001, incorporated trailer coaches from the aborted Class 210 DEMUs. It was used for testing and not general public service. Also at Potbridge, on a Basingstoke to Woking test run in January 1992, it carries standard NSE scheme 2 colours.

Right: The new standard EMUs for the South Eastern section were Classes 465 and 466. No 465004 is stabled at Clapham Junction in November 1992, showing the full NSE scheme 3 livery. The Class 466 is similar, but is a two-coach unit.

Above: At the LT open day at West Ruislip depot in May 1993, the brand-new Class 482 was on display, at this stage bereft of a unit number. The train is in a unique NSE colour scheme, and a Waterloo & City NSE logo and three-colour logo with Network South East wording can just be seen either side of the front passenger door. To photograph a Waterloo & City unit in the fresh air was an opportunity not to be missed!

Below: A pair of modern (sic) Class 483 Isle of Wight units leaves Ryde St John's Road on their way from Ryde Pierhead to Shanklin in June 1990. The front end details can be clearly seen, including the old LT 'A' end label ('D' at the other end). The red and white bands are brought up over the blue window frame area and extended back above it. Behind the white area above the cab windows, the roof is medium grey. The semaphore signal, NSE red lamppost and signalbox add to the scene for the modeller.

Above: The previous IoW incumbents were Classes 485 and 486 (4VEC and 3TIS). A part set of a Class 486 in localised NSE colours leaves Ryde Esplanade for Shanklin in August 1987. Note the black front window frames embellished with the IoW map and Ryde Rail wording in white, plus the NSE logo and full unit number. Ryde Rail is also under the white BR logo within the blue area at the front end.

Right: The older units on the Waterloo & City line were the ex-Southern Railway Class 487s. Unit 61 waits at Bank station ready to take off for Waterloo in November 1986. The ends of the coaches are not statutory yellow but white, as are the roofs, and there is a thin red band on the roof just clearing the sliding door opening. Note the BR logo, Network South East and logos as standard, but 'A' and presumably 'D' at the other end as LT standard.

Right: The Southern Region converted out-of-service EMUs for various departmental duties, an example here being a Class 930 converted from a Class 416 2EPB. Unit 005 is in NSE scheme 2 colours with abbreviated unit numbers over each front window and double headlights below the route panel. The unit is seen on Sandite circuit 43 to Virginia Water near Egham in October 1992.

Left: No 930062 was primarily an inter-depot stores unit, although it carries the caption 'The Sprinkler' above the unit number, indicating that it was probably also used for other purposes. But in May 1993, it was travelling from Eastleigh to Wimbledon as it passed Potbridge one evening. Note the sliding doors incorporated into the bodywork. Fitted with a single headlight, it is in NSE livery similar to Class 121 and 419 units, that is without swept-up ends.

Below: This Class 930 has been converted from a 4CEP Class 411 for route-learning duties and is thus fitted with three front windows. In addition, it carries double sets of headlights. In NSE scheme 2 colours, 3-coach No 930082 heads north out of Redhill in February 1996.

Above: Another route-learning unit was No 931001, converted from a later BR-built Class 416 2EPB. With four front windows and NSE scheme 2 colours, but with no NSE identification, it rounds the curve through Sandling station in July 1994. Again a single headlamp is fitted.

Right: Some Class 501 dc electric coaches were converted to battery units for use on lines when the current was cut off. An example is seen here at Hornsey depot in November 1988. 97707 is in NSE scheme 1 colours with white BR logo and Network South East wording plus NSE logo in the white band. The front end has been totally rebuilt with various lights, ladders, black window frames and a danger label, which is barely visible, warning of hydrogen gas! Almost all side windows have been replaced with louvres.

Above: The two versions of ScotRail locomotives are seen from above at Glasgow Queen Street in November 1988. No 47642 *Strathisla*, in the red striped version, complete with BR logo and Inverness Highland stag depot label, is waiting to depart for Inverness. No 47702 *Saint Cuthbert* is in the blue striped version with BR logo, and is bound for Edinburgh.

Left: The Class 47/7s were transferred to Network South East and fairly soon painted in its colours. One that held out was No 47706 which lost its ScotRail and BR logo identification, as well as its name, but did retain a small Eastfield Scottish terrier depot emblem. It also has an NSE logo between the marker lights. Working from Exeter to Waterloo and accelerating down the grade from Semley in October 1992, it will soon jam on the brakes for its stop at Tisbury.

Above: All the Class 47/7s were given blue stripes, but only one Class 47/4, namely No 47461 *Charles Rennie Mackintosh*. It is seen at Aldermaston in September 1988, working a Paddington to Paignton express, somewhat off its nominal beaten track! In the loop, a Class 33 waits for the road with a train of Bardon hoppers.

Below: No 47642 is seen again, but this time before being named. In red stripe ScotRail colours, it rounds the curve at East Linton in May 1986, making its way from Dunbar to Edinburgh with an evening service.

Above: Arriving at one of the platforms on the south side of Edinburgh Waverley, No 47492 *The Enterprising Scot* is at the end of a working from Poole. The loco carries an Inverness Highland stag depot logo and is in full red stripe ScotRail livery. The date is May 1987.

Below: Although No 47637 *Springburn* had been transferred to Old Oak Common by this time in April 1988, it still looks out of place smoking its way past Haslemere with a diverted Poole to Glasgow inter-regional express, especially since there is a genuine blue striped ScotRail coach behind the engine.

Right: Parcels sector No 08633 is well embellished with its nameplate '*The Sorter*' and the Crewe diesel depot Cheshire cat shed logo as it ambles through Crewe station in January 1994.

Right: This pairing, seen here in September 1991 at Stoford, was relatively rare on the LSWR main line to the South West. Parcels sector No 47712 *Lady Diana Spencer* pilots NSE No 50029 *Renown* with an Exeter to Waterloo express as it slams on the brakes to be able to stop at Yeovil Junction.

Below: The classic scene at Battledown as No 47703 *The Queen Mother* puts its foot down and accelerates under the flyover with a Waterloo to Exeter express in May 1993. Note the NSE logos under the number and between the marker lights.

Above: In April 1992, No 47642 displays the RES livery in ex-works condition as it passes Dringhouses on an ex-Doncaster running-in turn. Note the black roof with stone-coloured panel, brass BR logo on the offside cab, black cab doors with polished aluminium kick plates, OHE warning labels on the body side and front ends, and data panel. The light blue, black and red RES logo design is clearly seen in detail – it is more complex than perhaps first imagined.

Left: No 86401 hauls a train of empty charter stock towards Ledburn Junction in March 1992. Compared with No 47642 above, it does not appear to have any OHE warning labels or a BR logo, although it is otherwise in RES colours.

Below: A storm is brewing over London in July 1997. Presumably No 86253 *Manchester Guardian* has failed and RES No 90018 has been called on to work this Birmingham to Euston express, seen here at Headstone Lane. The dark sky highlights the colours, and the abbreviated number on the front end of the Class 90 can be seen. Ventilation panels cannot avoid breaking into the RES logo.

Above: The parcels sector operated a number of multiple-units; this one was somewhat different, having been rebuilt and restored to a green livery. Originally part of a Class 127 DMU and now numbered 920, the green colours are enhanced with thin yellow bands in the centre of the body and below the cantrail, a grey roof, BR crest and logo, two parcels (?) labels and the words Express Parcels. The roll-up access door is in aluminium. The front end has black-edged white 'go faster' wings and a black bird logo. It is passing Pengam in February 1989.

Below: A Class 114 is decked out in red and yellow in line with the wording carried on the body sides, namely Royal Mail Letters and the official Royal Mail logo. Two stripes are at the bottom of the body in yellow as is the coach number, but the BR logo is white. The roll-up doors are diagonally striped. As can be seen, the unit resides at Cambridge, and the date is March 1989.

Left: The Class 419s in Royal Mail colours were fairly uncommon, but here we see unit 9004 on the tail end of a Jaffa Cake Class 411 in Platform 1 on the eastern side of Victoria in March 1989. The train is destined for Dover Western Docks.

Below: Another DMU class used by the parcels sector was the 128, mainly on the Western Region. This example, No 55993 at Bescot in May 1990, is in similar colours to those on the Class 114, but the official Royal Mail logo with ER and the crown are better seen.

Bottom: The East Anglia Region used EMUs as well as DMUs for handling mail. Here we see No 302991 speeding past Stratford on its way to Liverpool Street in August 1993. It is in the same colours as those above, but carries a full unit number on the front end.

Miscellaneous and Non-Standard schemes

Right: Some units were painted in a scheme for Network North West as seen here on No 150207. The pale blue band of normal Provincial Sector colours has been replaced by red and green bands with the addition of a red and blue NNW logo and red BR logo. The train is entering Preston, having come from Liverpool, in July 1991.

Right: Stansted Express units have appeared in various schemes over the years, this first version being one of the cleanest in design. No 322485 creeps round the sharp curve into Bethnal Green on its way from the airport to Liverpool Street in August 1991

Below: When Gatwick Express operations were separated from Inter City, a livery very similar to IC was used. On the approach to Gatwick Airport, No 73201 *Broadlands* brings its designated service from Victoria past uninterested horses in this post-privatisation view in April 1996.

Left: Thameslink trains were painted in this original scheme (1) when first separated from Network South East. Full unit numbers were applied under the driver's window. In April 1996, No 319048 working a Bedford to Brighton fast service is arriving at Gatwick Airport.

Left: Although the next colour change to Thameslink (scheme 2) took place after privatisation, it was not a privatised livery as such. The black body with orange band was quite striking. No 319427 leaves Radlett in February 1998 on its way from Sutton to Luton.

Below: Eurostar was always a separate company and outside of the sectorisation structures but needs to be included for completeness. Class 373s were (and still are) painted in white and yellow. No 3004 is on its way from Waterloo to Brussels as it keeps to the speed limit round the bend at Tonbridge in August 1995.

Above: Stratford depot tarted up Class 08 No 08833 so as to look the part as Liverpool Street pilot. With Stratford, Painted Stratford TMD Oct 88 and Class 08 in white, and other white embellishments, it is the belle of the ball at the open day at Ilford in May 1989. Note the special colours on EMU No 302996 behind the 08, one of three GE region Sandite units.

Below: Poor No 33008 *Eastleigh* underwent three stages of repainting until it appeared in the correct original green, albeit with yellow warning panels. One of the intermediate stages is seen in October 1986 at Basingstoke as it heads a special from Waterloo to Yeovil Junction. The BR logo and the yellow strip above the cab windows are not original, and there should be a green strip between the yellow front panel and the white front window frame. The yellow panel is also too wide. However, it is still pleasant to see with its yellow ploughs and white wheel rims, even on a dull day.

Above: Only one locomotive was painted in Trans Pennine colours, namely No 47475. Entering York in October 1989, it is working its regular pattern with a Liverpool to Newcastle express.

Below: Four Class 47s were painted in Great Western green colours: Nos 47079 (which was a freight sector loco), 47484, 47500 and 47628. No 47500 *Great Western* is seen in close-up at Basingstoke, heading a Poole to Newcastle inter-regional express in March 1988. White wheel rims, yellow axlebox covers, silver buffers and red buffer beam add to the colour scheme. Compare this to the Voyagers now running the services!

Right: No 47522 *Doncaster Enterprise* carried this LNER-lookalike scheme before being repainted into parcels sector red. It stands at Bounds Green in November 1988. Note the Stratford cockney sparrow. When originally painted, it also carried the word Parcels next to the BR logo.

Above: This Class 47, numbered 97561 for a while, was decorated in an approximation of Crimson Lake to celebrate the 150th anniversary of the Midland Counties Railway after which it was named. Two days after its release, it worked a Derby-Swindon-Derby special, seen here on the return trip climbing the Lickey Incline in May 1989. With red buffer beam, white wheel rims and handrails, yellow axle boxes and silvered buffers it makes a splendid sight. Pity about the headboard.

Right: The original Class 50 was restored to BR blue and renumbered as D400. It is seen here in charge of an Exeter to Waterloo express leaving Yeovil Junction in June 1991.

Left: About to hammer over the points for the Exmouth branch, No 50007 *Sir Edward Elgar* passes the signalbox at Exmouth Junction with its service from Waterloo to Exeter in September 1990. The colours differ from the Class 47s decorated for GW150, in so far as the black and orange lining is only a strip along the body rather than being lined out around the bodyside. Note the remains of the EXJ facilites on the left of the picture.

Below: The full splendour of Pullman chocolate and cream can be seen on No 73101 as it stands in the yard at Stewarts Lane in November 1991. At this time the locomotive was named *Brighton Evening Argus*.

Left: In conjunction with GW150, Class 116 set B430 was painted in GW coaching stock colours. Working an Oxford to Reading stopping train, it is seen on a misty morning in November 1985 just south of Kennington Junction.

Above: The Class 142s allocated to the Western Region appeared in this travesty of Great Western coaching stock colours. Waiting to leave Plymouth for Gunnislake in June 1987, No 142027 is home to a small boy and not much else.

Below: The two Class 151s had their own version of Provincial Services colours as can be seen on unit 151001, which has arrived at Derby from Matlock in August 1986.

Left: Thumper unit 205029 was restored to plain green for its last days, with minimal embellishments and no details of an owner. The roof is silver. Waiting to depart from Penshurst in July 1993, it is working a Reigate to Tonbridge stopping train.

Below: To celebrate the ties between the Anglia Region and Dutch Railways, No 321334 was repainted into full NS colours. The unit number was positioned just above the hole for the coupling. It is seen at Stratford in August 1996 with a Liverpool Street to Southminster service.

Trains worked by non-Passenger and Parcels Sector locomotives

Right: The last days of the loco-hauled trains to Skegness saw pairs of Class 20s used, as seen here at Spondon in July 1992. No 20090 faces No 20132, both in Railfreight Red Stripe colours with a matched set of Regional Railways coaching stock, on a Derby to Skegness service.

Above: The attractive Wiltshire countryside around Tisbury is the setting for departmental-liveried No 33109 with its Waterloo to Exeter service in October 1992. This locomotive was always kept in quite smart condition with black front window frames and the Eastleigh Spitfire depot mascot plate.

Right: A Dutch livered example is illustrated by No 37010 with a train of mixed stock forming a Bristol to Weymouth service. The sleepy station of Yetminster plays host in August 1992. Note the metal BR logo below the number on the cab side.

Above: Another Bristol to Weymouth train is also in the hands of a Class 37. This time the loco is a Construction sector example, namely No 37425 *Sir Robert McAlpine/Concrete Bob*, approaching Bradford-on-Avon in August 1993.

Left: The Waterloo to Exeter services were, perforce, often in the hands of non-NSE locomotives for various reasons in the last years of loco haulage. This example shows a loco in a non-standard version of Railfreight, in so far as it carries a large BR logo with a small number in the middle of the bodyside. No 47370 *Thunderbird* is still accelerating away from Yeovil Junction on its way to the next stop at Sherborne as it passes the hamlet of Bradford Abbas in August 1992.

Right: A nice surprise for the photographer was the sight of the yellow infrastructure coloured Class 47 on a weekend Liverpool to Dover Western Docks inter-regional train. No 47803 is about to pass Swanley Junction in July 1993. In the days before mobile phones would summon all and sundry to the lineside for this, I was the only person on the footbridge!

Below: Even in the early days of privatisation, Saltley depot still had to cover for emergencies on trains from Edinburgh to the south. On Saturdays, the 09:10 from Edinburgh continued past Reading to Bournemouth, and having seen it at Lower Basildon, a quick drive could enable it to be seen again at Mortimer, as in this case where No 58017 *Eastleigh Depot* is in charge. It is August 1998, the loco is in Mainline grey, and a Virgin coach intrudes.

Left: Well into the privatised era, but looking almost as if it was at least seven years or so beforehand, Mainline blue No 73136 *Kent Youth Music* leads the Willesden to Dover mail train past Kensington Olympia in August 2001 (but EWS No 73131 on the back does give the game away about the date). Note the Stewarts Lane depot mascot plate on the 73, and the first and last vans which have lost their RES logos.

Below: Something has attracted the interest of the cab crew of No 90023 as it waits for a green to allow it to depart from King's Cross for Newcastle in February 1993. The engine is in Railfreight Distribution livery and compares with InterCity No 91002 which has arrived from Leeds. Note the metal BR logo on the Class 90.

Above: Strathclyde PTE units were dispersed to other areas as needed when new rolling stock made them surplus to day-to-day requirements. In this shot, No 101688 has moved to the East Midlands, where it is seen passing the old Great Central box at Retford Thrumpton with a Sheffield to Lincoln service in March 1993.

Right: The daffodils are in full bloom as Strathclyde No 107438 passes by with a Dundee to Arbroath train on the approaches to Broughty Ferry in March 1988. Not exactly a normal Strathclyde area working.

Above: Just pre-sectorisation, but as would have been for several more years, in full Strathclyde livery and very much on home ground, No 303307 leaves Milngavie for Springburn in April 1985. Modellers should note the dwarf semaphore signals.

Below: Tyne & Wear colours are clearly seen on No 143025 as it ticks over in Newcastle waiting for the signal to depart for Middlesbrough in June 1988.

Top: No 142019 was recorded as working a Newcastle Metrocentre to Middlesbrough service as it passed Pelaw in August 1993. The Tyne & Wear colours have Regional Railways wording added in the yellow band.

Above: An unidentified Class 141 in the original West Yorkshire PTE white with green band passes Poppleton Junction in April 1986 on its way from York to Leeds via Harrogate. Note the MetroTrain inscription and the pair of logos.

Right: In the later livery of red and white with yellow stripe, No 155344 passes Colton Junction with a York to Liverpool service in June 1989. The BR logo is now separate from the Metro-Train wording (note the hyphen) and M logo.

Above: The phrase 'short straw' comes to mind when seeing an ex-East Anglia Class 307 which was dumped on the West Riding. No 307122 waits at Doncaster in October 1990 before taking the road for Leeds.

Left: Only one unit was painted for the South Yorkshire PTE, seen here at Grantham whilst working a Nottingham to Skegness service in October 1984. The SYT logo can be seen, and the label commemorates 10 years of the PTE. *Gavin Morrison*

Below: A wet day at Guide Bridge (what a surprise!) and a Class 142 is being used for driver training. Passing the remains of the extensive layout that used to exist here, No 142006 heads west in April 1986, showing off its Greater Manchester PTE colour scheme with logos.

Above: Another of the ex-Strathclyde units to venture into new territory is seen in the stabling sidings at Stockport in April 1986. No 303067 carries the GMPTE colours but no M logo.

Below: On a route now operated by trams, Bury-bound Class 504 leaves Manchester Victoria on a sunny afternoon in July 1987. The M and BR logos are on the cab side, and the buffers carry some inventive hieroglyphics. These units never carried set numbers, only coach numbers as can be seen on the cab end.

Left: In the later GMPTE colours, also carrying Regional Railways wording, No 150217 leaves Liverpool Lime Street and enters the tunnel on its way to Preston in September 1993. The light stone and black bands are separated by red and white stripes.

Below: Merseyrail operated some DMUs as well as the extensive third rail EMU systems. In May 1993, No 150205 sat amongst the detritus of Manchester Piccadilly waiting to leave for New Mills.

Above: The island platform at Bidston sees No 508108 stop on its way from West Kirby to Liverpool in June 1994. Note the M logo on the station nameplate.

Below: Merseyrail received two Class 73s for working departmental trains when the power was switched off. 'JA' version No 73006 was stabled at Hall Road one evening in April 1994, and the Merseyrail M logo can be seen above the Regional Railways inscription.

Left: West Midlands PTE painted one EMU in the colours used by its road services, namely canary yellow and blue. The unit, No 312204, passes Bescot as it makes its way from Birmingham New Street to Walsall in February 1988. The unit number is in two sizes, a small class number and large unit number, and the WM logo is on the cab side, plus BR logo behind the cab door, both in white.

Below: Also seen at Bescot is No 310103 in a modified Provincial Services colour scheme, a dark blue band replacing the normal pale blue. The train is working a Walsall to Stoke-on-Trent service in June 1989. The logo incorporates both BR and WM liveries.

Right: In the more recent West Midlands colours of green, white and light blue, with yellow logos by the sliding doors, No 150115 is about to leave from the bay platform at Leamington Spa for Birmingham Snow Hill in July 1991.

Below: Very much a one-off was this three-tone blue bubble car, seen working a Barnt Green to Worcester train at Bromsgrove in July 1989. The unit carried a black number T133 on the front end and a large coach number 55033 in white. The Midline logo was augmented with BR and WM logos at each side. The yellow front end was swept in a diagonal form around the cab side. A very pretty little unit which would definitely add to a model layout.

Above: At the introduction of Network South East, but before coaches were painted in the new colours, logos and wording were applied as shown here on this Class 421.

Above: Class 442 2403 shows its Solent and Wessex NSE logo and The New Forest nameplate.

Above: For a short period, Class 421 units on the Central section were formed into pairs of semi-permanently coupled sets classed as 8DIG. They carried this 'Capital Coast Express' logo.

Above: Class 73s carried a variety of nameplates and badges. One of the most famous was No 73142 *Broadlands*, the nameplate featuring standard BR design lettering plus two badges.

Above: The script of the nameplate of No 73138 included two types; the Post Haste words were very much non-standard.

Above: Another nameplate using non-standard lettering was that of No 86429 *The Times*, which reflected the design used by the newspaper itself.

Above: At precisely 14:00 hours, GNER No 43106 erupts into life as it departs from King's Cross for Aberdeen. The stock is still in InterCity colours; the date is May 1997.

Below: A pair of RES Class 47s haul Virgin coaches on one of those Cross-Country services that has since disappeared. No 47741 *Resilient* tops the train; No 47769 *Resolve* tails it. The service was from Portsmouth & Southsea to Blackpool, and is seen near Chalton in April 2000.

Above: The pioneer South West Trains Class 442 2402 *County of Hants*, in its initial NSE scheme 3 livery plus orange band, works a Poole to Waterloo service past Eastleigh in July 1997, and also passes RTC Class 101 unit 19 Iris 2 in two-tone grey which is waiting to leave the shed lines.

Below: Locomotive-hauled parcels services ceased by 2006. As a memory of such services in recent times, EWS 67018 crawls round Langstone Rock in July 2000 with a Plymouth to Low Fell train.